PRESENTED TO

_____

FROM

D1072267

_____

DATE

_____

DECEMBER 31

So you also have sorrow now.
But I will see you again.
Your hearts will rejoice,
and no one will rob you of your joy.

JOHN 16:22 HCSB

DECEMBER 30

The resurrection of Jesus, the whole alphabet
of human hope, the certificate of our Lord's mission
from heaven, is the heart of the gospel in all ages.

R. G. LEE

Amazing grace, how sweet the sound,
That saved a wretch like me!
I once was lost, but now am found,
Was blind, but now I see.

Amazing Grace
JOHN NEWTON
1725–1807

DECEMBER 29

It is my Father's will that all who see His Son and believe in Him should have eternal life. I will raise them up at the last day.

JOHN 6:40 NLT

JANUARY 2

For you are saved by grace through faith,
and this is not from yourselves; it is God's gift—
not from works, so that no one can boast.

EPHESIANS 2:8–9 HCSB

DECEMBER 28

When we slow down and express our gratitude
to the One who made us, we enrich our own lives
and the lives of those around us. Whatever
your circumstances—whether you're sitting
on the front porch, or anywhere else for that matter—
slow down and express your thanks to the Creator.

JANUARY 3

Whether your style is country-fried or citified,
high-fashion or no-fashion, grits or gourmet,
God's grace is absolutely free for the asking,
paid for in full. No shoes, no shirt, no problem—
He loves you just as you are.

DECEMBER 27

He is not here, but He has been resurrected!

LUKE 24:6 HCSB

JANUARY 4

My grace is sufficient for you,
for My power is made perfect in weakness.

2 CORINTHIANS 12:9 NIV

For I delivered to you first of all that which I also received:
that Christ died for our sins according to the Scriptures,
and that He was buried, and that He rose again
the third day according to the Scriptures.

1 CORINTHIANS 15:3–4 NKJV

God is the giver, and we are the receivers. And His richest gifts are bestowed not upon those who do the greatest things, but upon those who accept His abundance and His grace.

HANNAH WHITALL SMITH

DECEMBER 25

Praise be to the God and Father of our Lord Jesus Christ!
In His great mercy He has given us new birth
into a living hope through the resurrection
of Jesus Christ from the dead.

1 PETER 1:3 NIV

So I'll cherish the old rugged cross,
Till my trophies at last I lay down;
I will cling to the old rugged cross,
And exchange it some day for a crown.

Old Rugged Cross
GEORGE BENNARD
1915

Christ the Lord is risen today, Alleluia!
Earth and heaven in chorus say, Alleluia!
Raise your joys and triumphs high, Alleluia!
Sing, ye heavens, and earth reply, Alleluia!

Christ the Lord Is Risen Today
CHARLES WESLEY
1707-1788

Greater love has no one than this,
than to lay down one's life for his friends.

JOHN 15:13 NKJV

Then Jesus spoke to them again: "I am the light of the world. Anyone who follows Me will never walk in the darkness, but will have the light of life."

JOHN 8:12 HCSB

I am the good shepherd. The good shepherd lays down his life for the sheep.

JOHN 10:11 NIV

DECEMBER 22

A disciple is a follower of Christ. That means
you take on His priorities as your own.
His agenda becomes your agenda.
His mission becomes your mission.

CHARLES STANLEY

This is love: not that we loved God,
but that He loved us and sent His Son
as an atoning sacrifice for our sins.

1 JOHN 4:10 NIV

Be imitators of God,
as beloved children.

EPHESIANS 5:1 NASB

Christ shed His blood for you. He will walk with you through this life and throughout all eternity. So today, as you say your prayers and count your blessings, think about His sacrifice and His grace. And be thankful.

DECEMBER 20

When we're in the friendly surroundings of our
local church, it's easier to talk about Christ's
transforming power and His never-ending love.
But once we've left the security of the church setting,
talking about Jesus can be more difficult. Nonetheless,
God wants us to share His Good News with the world.

JANUARY 11

For when we were yet without strength,
in due time Christ died for the ungodly.

ROMANS 5:6 KJV

How happy is everyone who fears the Lord,
who walks in His ways!

PSALM 128:1 HCSB

God proved His love on the cross.
When Christ hung, and bled, and died
it was God saying to the world, "I love you."

BILLY GRAHAM

DECEMBER 18

"Follow Me," Jesus told them, "and I will make you fish for people!" Immediately they left their nets and followed Him.

MARK 1:17–18 HCSB

For God so loved the world, that He gave His only begotten Son, that whosoever believeth in Him should not perish, but have everlasting life.

JOHN 3:16 KJV

Whoever wants to save his life will lose it,
but whoever loses his life because of Me
and the gospel will save it.

MARK 8:35 HCSB

Gimme that old time religion.
Gimme that old time religion.
Gimme that old time religion.
It's good enough for me.

OLD TIME RELIGION TRADITIONAL SPIRITUAL

DECEMBER 16

There is a name I love to hear, I love to sing its worth.
It sounds like music in my ear, the sweetest name on earth.
O how I love Jesus, O how I love Jesus,
O how I love Jesus, because he first loved me!

O How I Love Jesus
FREDERICK WHITFIELD
1855

Don't be afraid, because I am your God.
I will make you strong and will help you;
I will support you with My right hand that saves you.

ISAIAH 41:10 NCV

Let us run the race that is before us and never give up.
We should remove from our lives anything that would
get in the way and the sin that so easily holds us back.

HEBREWS 12:1 NCV

For truly I say to you, if you have faith the size
of a mustard seed, you will say to this mountain,
"Move from here to there" and it will move;
and nothing will be impossible to you.

MATTHEW 17:20 NASB

Great accomplishments are often attempted
but only occasionally reached. Those who reach them
are usually those who have missed many times before.

CHARLES SWINDOLL

Don't be afraid. Only believe.

MARK 5:36 HCSB

DECEMBER 13

You have need of endurance,
so that when you have done the will of God,
you may receive what was promised.

HEBREWS 10:36 NASB

Back in the country, old-time religion hasn't gone out of style. The simple faith that energized Paul, Silas, and countless other members of the early church is still moving mountains today. Their faith enabled them to move mountains, and you can move mountains, if you have faith.

If you're enduring tough times, remember that every marathon has a finish line, and so does yours. So keep putting one foot in front of the other, pray for strength, and don't give up. Whether you realize it or not, you're up to the challenge if you persevere.

Blessed are they that have not seen,
and yet have believed.

JOHN 20:29 KJV

DECEMBER 11

Finishing is better than starting.
Patience is better than pride.

ECCLESIASTES 7:8 NLT

I beg you to recognize the extreme simplicity of faith;
it is nothing more nor less than just believing God
when He says He either has done something for us,
or will do it; and then trusting Him to do it.
It is so simple that it is hard to explain.

HANNAH WHITALL SMITH

Let us not become weary in doing good,
for at the proper time we will reap a harvest
if we do not give up.

GALATIANS 6:9 NIV

All things are possible
for the one who believes.

MARK 9:23 NCV

DECEMBER 9

But as for you, be strong;
don't be discouraged,
for your work has a reward.

2 CHRONICLES 15:7 HCSB

JANUARY 22

What a friend we have in Jesus,
all our sins and griefs to bear!
What a privilege to carry everything to God in prayer!
O what peace we often forfeit,
O what needless pain we bear,
All because we do not carry everything to God in prayer!

JOSEPH M. SCRIVEN
1855

Heard the voice of Jesus say,
Come unto me I am the way.
Keep your hand on the plow, hold on.
When my way get dark as night,
I know the Lord will be my light.
Keep your hand on the plow, hold on.

Hold On (Keep Your Hand on the Plow)
TRADITIONAL SPIRITUAL

I am the good shepherd. The good shepherd lays down his life for the sheep.

JOHN 10:11 HCSB

This is My commandment,
that you love one another
as I have loved you.

JOHN 15:12 NKJV

As the Father loved Me, I also have loved you;
abide in My love.

JOHN 15:9 NKJV

The mind of Christ is to be learned in the family.
Strength of character may be acquired at work,
but beauty of character is learned at home.

HENRY DRUMMOND

No one has greater love than this, that someone would lay down his life for his friends.

JOHN 15:13 HCSB

Above all, put on love—the perfect bond of unity.

COLOSSIANS 3:14 HCSB

Jesus is, quite simply, the best friend this world has ever known. Jesus loves us so much that He willingly sacrificed Himself on the cross so that we might live with Him throughout eternity.

His love endures. Even when we falter, He loves us. When we fall prey to the world's temptations, He remains steadfast. In fact, no power on earth can separate us from His love.

DECEMBER 4

A happy home is a treasure from God.
If the Lord has blessed you with a close-knit family
and a peaceful home, give thanks to your Creator
because He has given you one of His
most precious earthy possessions.

For Christ also suffered once for sins,
the just for the unjust,
that He might bring us to God,
being put to death in the flesh
but made alive by the Spirit.

1 PETER 3:18 NKJV

DECEMBER 3

Love each other like brothers and sisters.
Give each other more honor
than you want for yourselves.

ROMANS 12:10 NCV

Jesus can be your friend if you let Him,
when you bring Him close, when you make Him
an important part of your life.

TENNESSEE ERNIE FORD

Choose for yourselves today the one you will worship....
As for me and my family, we will worship Yahweh.

JOSHUA 24:15 HCSB

We love Him, because He first loved us.

1 JOHN 4:19 KJV

He blesses the home of the righteous.

PROVERBS 3:33 NIV

I sing because I'm happy, (I'm happy)
I sing because I'm free, (I'm free)
For His eye is on the sparrow,
And I know He watches me.

His Eye Is on the Sparrow
CIVILLA D. MARTIN AND CHARLES H. GABRIEL
1905

'Mid pleasures and palaces tho' we may roam,
Be it ever so humble, there's no place like home.
A charm from the skies seems to hallow us there,
Which, seek thro' the world, is ne'er met with elsewhere.
Home, home, sweet, sweet home,
Be it ever so humble, there's no place like home.

Home, Sweet Home
JOHN HOWARD PAYNE
1791-1852

The Lord is my shepherd, I shall not want.
He makes me lie down in green pastures;
He leads me beside quiet waters. He restores my soul.

PSALM 23:1–3 NASB

I remind you to fan into flame the gift of God.

2 TIMOTHY 1:6 NIV

FEBRUARY 1

The Lord is my light and my salvation—
whom should I fear?
The Lord is the stronghold of my life—
of whom should I be afraid?

PSALM 27:1 HCSB

NOVEMBER 28

God has given you special talents—
now it's your turn to give them back to God.

MARIE T. FREEMAN

As for God, His way is perfect;
the word of the Lord is proven;
He is a shield to all who trust in Him.

Every good and perfect gift is from above,
coming down from the Father of the heavenly lights,
who does not change like shifting shadows.

JAMES 1:17 NIV

FEBRUARY 3

When every earthly support system fails, God remains
steadfast, and His love remains unchanged.
When we encounter life's inevitable disappointments
and setbacks, the Father remains faithful.
When we suffer, He is always there for us, always ready
to respond to our prayers, always working in us
and through us to turn tragedy into triumph.

All your talents, all your opportunities, and all your gifts are on temporary loan from the Creator. Use those gifts while you can because time is short and the needs are great. In every undertaking, make God your partner. Then, just as He promised, God will bless you now and forever.

FEBRUARY 4

Those who trust in the Lord are like Mount Zion.
It cannot be shaken; it remains forever.

PSALM 125:1 HCSB

NOVEMBER 25

There are diversities of gifts,
but the same Spirit.

1 CORINTHIANS 12:4 KJV

Faith is not merely holding on to God.
It is God holding on to you.

CORRIE TEN BOOM

NOVEMBER 24

Do not neglect the gift that is in you.

1 TIMOTHY 4:14 NKJV

So we may boldly say: "The Lord is my helper; I will not fear. What can man do to me?"

HEBREWS 13:6 NKJV

NOVEMBER 23

God has given each of you a gift from His great variety of spiritual gifts. Use them well to serve one another.

1 PETER 4:10 NLT

FEBRUARY 7

Said the Robin to the Sparrow,
"I should really like to know
Why these anxious human beings
rush about and worry so."

Said the Sparrow to the Robin,
"Friend I think that it must be
that they have no Heavenly Father
such as cares for you and me."

Overheard In an Orchard
ELIZABETH CHANEY
1859

But the Master comes,
And the foolish crowd never can quite understand,
The worth of a soul and the change that is wrought
By the Touch of the Masters' Hand.

The Touch of the Master's Hand
MYRA BROOKS WELCH
1921

Cast all your anxiety on Him
because He cares for you.

1 PETER 5:7 NIV

When you talk, do not say harmful things,
but say what people need—words that will help others
become stronger. Then what you say will do good
to those who listen to you.

EPHESIANS 4:29 NCV

Therefore do not worry about tomorrow,
for tomorrow will worry about its own things.
Sufficient for the day is its own trouble.

MATTHEW 6:34 NKJV

Discouraged people don't need critics.
They hurt enough already. They don't need
more guilt or piled-on distress.
They need encouragement. They need a refuge,
a willing, caring, available someone.

CHARLES SWINDOLL

Peace I leave with you; My peace I give to you;
not as the world gives do I give to you.
Do not let your heart be troubled, nor let it be fearful.

JOHN 14:27 NASB

NOVEMBER 19

So encourage each other and give each other strength,
just as you are doing now.

1 THESSALONIANS 5:11 NCV

God has promised that we may lead lives of abundance, not anxiety. In fact, His Word instructs us to "be anxious for nothing." But how can we put our fears to rest? By taking those fears to Him and leaving them there.

NOVEMBER 18

Whom will you encourage today? How many times
will you share a smile, or a kind word, or a pat
on the back? You'll probably have many opportunities
to share the gift of encouragement. When you seize
those opportunities, others will be blessed,
and you'll be blessed, too.

Do not be anxious about anything, but in everything,
by prayer and petition, with thanksgiving,
present your requests to God.

PHILIPPIANS 4:6 NIV

NOVEMBER 17

Bear one another's burdens,
and so fulfill the law of Christ.

GALATIANS 6:2 NKJV

What you trust to Him you must not worry over nor feel anxious about. Trust and worry cannot go together.

HANNAH WHITALL SMITH

NOVEMBER 16

Encourage each other daily, while it is still called today, so that none of you is hardened by sin's deception.

HEBREWS 3:13 HCSB

Cast your burden on the Lord,
And He shall sustain you;
He shall never permit the righteous to be moved.

PSALM 55:22 NKJV

NOVEMBER 15

Let us think about each other and help each other
to show love and do good deeds.

HEBREWS 10:24 NCV

Swing low, sweet chariot,
Coming for to carry me home.
Swing low, sweet chariot,
Coming for to carry me home.

Swing Low, Sweet Chariot
TRADITIONAL SPIRITUAL

NOVEMBER 14

There are hermit souls that live withdrawn
In the place of their self-content;
There are souls like stars, that dwell apart,
In a fellowless firmament;
There are pioneer souls that blaze their paths
Where highways never ran—
But let me live by the side of the road
And be a friend to man.

The House by the Side of the Road
SAM WALTER FOSS
1858-1911

For God so loved the world, that He gave
His only begotten Son, that whosoever believeth in Him
should not perish, but have everlasting life.

JOHN 3:16 KJV

NOVEMBER 13

He who sat on the throne said,
"Behold, I make all things new."

REVELATION 21:5 NKJV

Rejoice and be exceedingly glad,
for great is your reward in heaven.

MATTHEW 5:12 NKJV

The world changes—circumstances change, we change—but God's Word never changes.

WARREN WIERSBE

Most assuredly, I say to you, he who hears My word
and believes in Him who sent Me has everlasting life,
and shall not come into judgment,
but has passed from death into life.

JOHN 5:24 NKJV

NOVEMBER 11

God, create a clean heart for me
and renew a steadfast spirit within me.

PSALM 51:10 HCSB

Jesus has overcome the troubles of this world.
We should trust Him, and we should obey
His commandments. When we do, we can withstand
any problem, knowing that our troubles
are temporary, but that heaven is not.

Even in sleepy small towns, things change.
People change; surroundings change;
technologies change; even habits change.
It's simply a fact of life: the world keeps changing
and so do we. Thankfully, God doesn't change.
And neither do His promises.

You have this faith and love because of your hope, and what you hope for is kept safe for you in heaven. You learned about this hope when you heard the message about the truth, the Good News.

COLOSSIANS 1:5 NCV

NOVEMBER 9

Grow in the grace and knowledge of our Lord
and Savior Jesus Christ. To Him be the glory
both now and forever. Amen.

2 PETER 3:18 NKJV

If you are a Christian, you are not a citizen
of this world trying to get to heaven; you are a citizen
of heaven making your way through this world.

VANCE HAVNER

NOVEMBER 8

To every thing there is a season,
and a time to every purpose under the heaven.

ECCLESIASTES 3:1 KJV

FEBRUARY 22

For now we see in a mirror, dimly,
but then face to face. Now I know in part,
but then I shall know just as I also am known.

1 CORINTHIANS 13:12 NKJV

The wise see danger ahead and avoid it,
but fools keep going and get into trouble.

PROVERBS 22:3 NCV

I love to tell the story;
'Twill be my theme in glory
To tell the old, old story
Of Jesus and His love.

I Love to Tell the Story
KATHERINE HANKEY
1866

Time is filled with swift transition,
Naught of earth unmoved can stand,
Build your hopes on things eternal,
Hold to God's unchanging hand.

Hold to God's Unchanging Hand
JENNIE B. WILSON
1906

I say to you, anyone who acknowledges Me before men,
the Son of Man will also acknowledge him
before the angels of God.

LUKE 12:8 HCSB

Morning by morning He wakens me
and opens my understanding to His will.
The Sovereign Lord has spoken to me,
and I have listened.

ISAIAH 50:4–5 NLT

God has not given us a spirit of fear and timidity, but of power, love, and self-discipline. So never be ashamed to tell others about our Lord.

2 TIMOTHY 1:7–8 NLT

God's guidance is even more important than common sense.
I can declare that the deepest darkness
is outshone by the light of Jesus.

CORRIE TEN BOOM

You must worship Christ as Lord of your life.
And if someone asks about your Christian hope,
always be ready to explain it.

1 PETER 3:15 NLT

NOVEMBER 3

Show me Thy ways, O Lord; teach me Thy paths.
Lead me in Thy truth, and teach me: for Thou art
the God of my salvation; on Thee do I wait all the day.

PSALM 25:4–5 KJV

We live in a world that desperately needs the healing message of Jesus Christ. And, every believer, each in his or her own way, bears a personal responsibility for sharing that message. If you've been transformed by God's only begotten Son, now it's your turn to share His truth with others.

When we ask for God's guidance, with our hearts and minds open to His direction, He will lead us along a path of His choosing. Trust God's promises and talk to Him often. When you do, He'll guide your steps today, tomorrow, and forever.

All those who stand before others
and say they believe in Me,
I will say before My Father in heaven
that they belong to Me.

MATTHEW 10:32 NCV

NOVEMBER 1

Teach me to do Your will, for You are my God;
Your Spirit is good. Lead me in the land of uprightness.

PSALM 143:10 NKJV

His voice leads us not into timid discipleship
but into bold witness.

CHARLES STANLEY

Trust in the Lord with all your heart,
and lean not on your own understanding;
in all your ways acknowledge Him,
and He shall direct your paths.

PROVERBS 3:5–6 NKJV

He said to them, "Go into all the world
and preach the gospel to the whole creation."

MARK 16:15 HCSB

Yet Lord, You are our Father;
we are the clay, and You are our potter;
we all are the work of Your hands.

ISAIAH 64:8 HCSB

When the roll is called up yonder, When the roll
is called up yonder, When the roll is called up yonder,
When the roll is called up yonder, I'll be there.

When the Roll Is Called Up Yonder
JAMES MILTON BLACK
1893

Jesus, Savior, pilot me
Over life's tempestuous sea;
Unknown waves before me roll,
Hiding rock and treach'rous shoal.
Chart and compass come from Thee.
Jesus, Savior, pilot me.

Jesus, Savior, Pilot Me
EDWARD HOPPER
1871

I am the resurrection and the life. The one who believes in Me will live, even though they die; and whoever lives by believing in Me will never die.

JOHN 11:25–26 NIV

Blessings crown the head of the righteous.

PROVERBS 10:6 NIV

For God so loved the world, that He gave His only begotten Son, that whosoever believeth in Him should not perish, but have everlasting life.

JOHN 3:16 KJV

God is the giver, and we are the receivers.
And His richest gifts are bestowed not upon those
who do the greatest things, but upon those
who accept His abundance and His grace.

HANNAH WHITALL SMITH

I tell you the truth,
anyone who believes
has eternal life.

JOHN 6:47 NLT

The Lord is my shepherd;
I shall not want.

PSALM 23:1 KJV

MARCH 6

Ours is not a distant God. He is always present,
always ready to guide and protect us.
He watches over His creation and He understands—
far better than we ever could—
the essence of what it means to be human.

Your blessings, all of which are gifts from above, are indeed too numerous to count, but it never hurts to begin counting them anyway. It never hurts to say thanks to the Giver for the gifts you can count, and all the other ones, too.

Sing to the Lord, all the earth;
proclaim His salvation day after day.

1 CHRONICLES 16:23 NIV

The Lord is my rock, my fortress, and my deliverer,
my God, my mountain where I seek refuge.
My shield, the horn of my salvation, my stronghold,
my refuge, and my Savior.

2 SAMUEL 22:2–3 HCSB

Conversion may take place in a second of time,
and so may restoration.

C. H. SPURGEON

OCTOBER 23

May Yahweh bless you and protect you;
may Yahweh make His face shine on you
and be gracious to you.

NUMBERS 6:24–25 HCSB

The Lord is my strength and my song;
He has become my salvation.

EXODUS 15:2 HCSB

OCTOBER 22

You will show me the path of life;
in Your presence is fullness of joy;
at Your right hand are pleasures forevermore.

PSALM 16:11 NKJV

MARCH 10

Isn't it strange, that princes and kings,
And clowns that caper in sawdust rings,
And common-folk like you and me,
Are builders for eternity?

A Bag of Tools
R.L. SHARPE
c. 1809

OCTOBER 21

When upon life's billows you are tempest tossed,
When you are discouraged, thinking all is lost,
Count your many blessings, name them one by one,
And it will surprise you what the Lord hath done.

Count Your Blessings
JOHN OATMAN, JR.
1897

MARCH 11

Shepherd God's flock, for whom you are responsible.
Watch over them because you want to,
not because you are forced. That is how God wants it.
Do it because you are happy to serve.

1 PETER 5:2 NCV

These things I have spoken to you, that in Me you may have peace. In the world you will have tribulation; but be of good cheer, I have overcome the world.

JOHN 16:33 NKJV

The greatest among you must be a servant.
But those who exalt themselves will be humbled,
and those who humble themselves will be exalted.

MATTHEW 23:11–12 NLT

Jesus did not promise to change the circumstances around us. He promised great peace and pure joy to those who would learn to believe that God actually controls all things.

CORRIE TEN BOOM

MARCH 13

As each one has received a gift,
minister it to one another, as good stewards
of the manifold grace of God.

1 PETER 4:10 NKJV

"I will give peace, real peace, to those far and near, and I will heal them," says the Lord.

ISAIAH 57:19 NCV

MARCH 14

Jesus came to this world, not to conquer, but to serve.
We must do likewise by helping those who cannot help
themselves. When we do, our lives will be blessed
by the One who first served us.

Have you discovered the genuine peace that can be yours through Christ? Or are you still pursuing the illusion of peace that the world promises but cannot deliver? If you've turned things over to Jesus, you'll be blessèd. And you'll experience the only peace that really matters: God's peace.

MARCH 15

Blessed are those servants, whom the Lord
when He cometh shall find watching.

LUKE 12:37 KJV

The fruit of the Spirit is love, joy, peace, patience, kindness, goodness, faith, gentleness, self-control. Against such things there is no law.

GALATIANS 5:22-23 HCSB

The measure of a life, after all,
is not its duration but its donation.

CORRIE TEN BOOM

OCTOBER 15

Peace I leave with you, My peace I give to you; not as the world gives do I give to you. Let not your heart be troubled, neither let it be afraid.

JOHN 14:27 NKJV

MARCH 17

Assuredly, I say to you, inasmuch as you
did it to one of the least of these My brethren,
you did it to Me.

MATTHEW 25:40 NKJV

The peace of God, which passeth all understanding, shall keep your hearts and minds through Christ Jesus.

PHILIPPIANS 4:7 KJV

Standing on the promises of Christ my king,
Through eternal ages let his praises ring;
Glory in the highest, I will shout and sing,
Standing on the promises of God.

Standing on the Promises
RUSSELL KELSO CARTER
1886

OCTOBER 13

I need thee every hour, most gracious Lord;
No tender voice like thine can peace afford.
I need thee, O I need thee, every hour I need thee.
O bless me now, my Savior; I come to thee.

I Need Thee Every Hour
ANNIE S. HAWKS AND ROBERT LOWERY
1872

Sustain me as You promised, and I will live;
do not let me be ashamed of my hope.

PSALM 119:116 HCSB

Be strong and courageous,
all you who put your hope in the Lord.

PSALM 31:24 HCSB

Let us hold on to the confession of our hope without wavering, for He who promised is faithful.

HEBREWS 10:23 HCSB

Darkness may throw a shadow over my outer vision,
but there is no cloud that can keep
the sunlight of hope from a trustful soul.

FANNY CROSBY

As for God, His way is perfect:
the word of the Lord is tried:
He is a buckler to all those that trust in Him.

PSALM 18:30 KJV

The Lord is good to those who wait for Him, to the soul who seeks Him. It is good that one should hope and wait quietly for the salvation of the Lord.

LAMENTATIONS 3:25-26 NKJV

When we accept Christ into our hearts, God promises us the opportunity to experience contentment, peace, and spiritual abundance. But more importantly, God promises that the priceless gift of eternal life will be ours. These promises should give us comfort. With God on our side, we have absolutely nothing to fear in this world and everything to hope for in the next.

God's promises give us hope: hope for today, hope for tomorrow, hope for all eternity. The hope that the world offers is temporary, at best. But the hope that God offers never grows old and never goes out of date. It's no wonder, then, that when we pin our hopes to worldly resources, we are often disappointed. Thankfully, God has no such record of failure.

My God is my rock, in whom I take refuge,
my shield and the horn of my salvation.

2 SAMUEL 22:3 NIV

OCTOBER 8

I say to myself, "The Lord is mine,
so I hope in Him."

LAMENTATIONS 3:24 NCV

From one end of the Bible to the other,
God assures us that He will never
go back on His promises.

BILLY GRAHAM

Let us hold fast the confession of our hope without wavering, for He who promised is faithful.

HEBREWS 10:23 NASB

He heeded their prayer,
because they put their trust in Him.

1 CHRONICLES 5:20 NKJV

OCTOBER 6

This hope we have as an anchor of the soul,
a hope both sure and steadfast.

HEBREWS 6:19 NASB

Rock of Ages, cleft for me,
let me hide myself in thee;
Let the water and the blood,
from thy wounded side which flowed,
Be of sin the double cure;
save from wrath and make me pure.

Rock of Ages
AUGUSTUS MONTAGUE TOPLADY
1763

Soft as the voice of an angel, breathing a lesson unheard,
Hope with a gentle persuasion whispers her comforting word:
Wait till the darkness is over, wait till the tempest is done,
Hope for the sunshine tomorrow, after the shower is gone.

Whispering Hope
SEPTIMUS WINNER
1868

MARCH 27

Be on guard. Stand firm in the faith.
Be courageous. Be strong.

1 CORINTHIANS 16:13 NLT

From the rising of the sun to its setting,
the name of the Lord is to be praised.

PSALM 113:3 NASB

The Lord is my rock and my fortress and my deliverer;
My God, my strength, in whom I will trust;
My shield and the horn of my salvation, my stronghold.

PSALM 18:2 NKJV

OCTOBER 3

The best moment to praise God
is always the present one.

MARIE T. FREEMAN

MARCH 29

God has not given us a spirit of fearfulness,
but one of power, love, and sound judgment.

2 TIMOTHY 1:7 HCSB

The Lord is my strength and my song;
He has become my salvation.

EXODUS 15:2 HCSB

When you form a one-on-one relationship
with your Creator, you can be comforted by the fact
that wherever you find yourself, whether at the top
of the mountain or the depths of the valley, God is there
with you. And because your Creator cares for you
and protects you, you can rise above your fears.

OCTOBER 1

If you sincerely desire to be a worthy servant
of the One who has given you eternal love
and eternal life, praise Him for who He is
and for what He has done for you.
Praise Him throughout the day, every day,
for as long as you live…and then for all eternity.

MARCH 31

I can do all things through Him
who strengthens me.

PHILIPPIANS 4:13 NASB

SEPTEMBER 30

At the name of Jesus every knee should bow,
of things in heaven, and things in earth,
and things under the earth; and that every tongue
should confess that Jesus Christ is Lord,
to the glory of God the Father.

PHILIPPIANS 2:10–11 KJV

The Rock of Ages is the great sheltering encirclement.

OSWALD CHAMBERS

Let everything that breathes praise the Lord.
Hallelujah!

PSALM 150:6 HCSB

Behold, God is my salvation;
I will trust, and not be afraid.

ISAIAH 12:2 KJV

In everything give thanks; for this is the will of God in Christ Jesus for you.

1 THESSALONIANS 5:18 NKJV

Just a closer walk with Thee.
Grant it, Jesus, is my plea
Daily walking close to Thee,
Let it be, dear Lord, let it be.

Just a Closer Walk with Thee
TRADITIONAL SPIRITUAL

All hail the power of Jesus' name!
Let angels prostrate fall.
Bring forth the royal diadem,
and crown him Lord of all.
Bring forth the royal diadem,
and crown him Lord of all!

All Hail the Power of Jesus' Name
EDWARD PERRONET
1779

But whoever keeps His word, truly in him
the love of God is perfected. This is how we know
we are in Him: the one who says he remains in Him
should walk just as He walked.

1 JOHN 2:5–6 HCSB

Therefore if anyone is in Christ, he is a new creation;
the old things have passed away, and look,
new things have come.

2 CORINTHIANS 5:17 HCSB

APRIL 5

Then He said to them all, "If anyone wants
to come with Me, he must deny himself,
take up his cross daily, and follow Me."

LUKE 9:23 HCSB

Be filled with the Holy Spirit; join a church
where the members believe the Bible and know the Lord;
seek the fellowship of other Christians; learn and
be nourished by God's Word and His many promises.
Conversion is not the end of your journey—
it is only the beginning.

CORRIE TEN BOOM

Walk in a manner worthy of the God who calls you into His own kingdom and glory.

1 THESSALONIANS 2:12 NASB

When we were baptized, we were buried
with Christ and shared His death.
So, just as Christ was raised from the dead
by the wonderful power of the Father,
we also can live a new life.

ROMANS 6:4 NCV

Today, do your part to take up the cross
and follow Jesus, even if the world encourages you
to do otherwise. When you're traveling step-by-step
with the Son of God, you're always on the right path.

As Christians, we are called to share
the Good News of Jesus Christ with our families,
with our neighbors, and with the world.
Jesus commanded His disciples to become fishers
of men. We have the honor of doing likewise.

Take My yoke upon you, and learn of Me;
for I am meek and lowly in heart:
and ye shall find rest unto your souls.
For My yoke is easy, and My burden is light.

MATTHEW 11:29–30 KJV

You have been born again, and this new life did not come from something that dies, but from something that cannot die. You were born again through God's living message that continues forever.

1 PETER 1:23 NCV

This is my song through endless ages:
Jesus led me all the way.

FANNY CROSBY

I preached that they should repent and turn to God
and prove their repentance by their deeds.

ACTS 26:20 NIV

Whoever is not willing to carry the cross and follow Me is not worthy of Me. Those who try to hold on to their lives will give up true life. Those who give up their lives for Me will hold on to true life.

MATTHEW 10:38–39 NCV

Everyone who calls
on the name of the Lord
will be saved.

ROMANS 10:13 HCSB

Just as I am, without one plea,
But that thy blood was shed for me,
And that thou bidd'st me come to thee,
O Lamb of God, I come, I come.

Just As I Am
CHARLOTTE ELLIOT
1835

SEPTEMBER 19

We praise Thee, O God!
For the Son of Thy love,
For Jesus who died,
And is now gone above.
Hallelujah! Thine the glory.
Hallelujah! Amen.

Revive Us Again
WILLIAM P. MACKAY
1839-1885

He is gracious and compassionate,
slow to anger, rich in faithful love.

JOEL 2:13 HCSB

He who follows righteousness and mercy finds life,
righteousness, and honor.

PROVERBS 21:21 NKJV

And we have known and believed the love
that God has for us. God is love, and he who abides
in love abides in God, and God in him.

1 JOHN 4:16 NKJV

Holiness, not happiness,
is the chief end of man.

OSWALD CHAMBERS

APRIL 14

For God so loved the world, that He gave
His only begotten Son, that whosoever believeth in Him
should not perish, but have everlasting life.

JOHN 3:16 KJV

SEPTEMBER 16

The highway of the upright avoids evil;
the one who guards his way protects his life.

PROVERBS 16:17 HCSB

God's grace is sufficient to meet our every need.
No matter our circumstances, no matter our personal
histories, the Lord's precious gifts are always available.
All we need to do is form a personal, life-altering
relationship with His only begotten Son,
and we're secure, now and forever.

The Holy Bible contains careful instructions which, if followed, lead to fulfillment and salvation. But, if we choose to ignore God's commandments, the results are as predictable as they are tragic. So if you'd like a simple, surefire formula for abundant living, here it is: live righteously. And for further instructions, read the manual.

APRIL 16

Give thanks to Him and praise His name.
For Yahweh is good, and His love is eternal;
His faithfulness endures through all generations.

PSALM 100:4–5 HCSB

SEPTEMBER 14

Seek first the kingdom of God and His righteousness,
and all these things shall be added to you.

MATTHEW 6:33 NKJV

How beautiful it is to learn that grace isn't fragile,
and that in the family of God
we can fail and not be a failure.

GLORIA GAITHER

Live peaceful and quiet lives
in all godliness and holiness.

1 TIMOTHY 2:2 NIV

APRIL 18

The Lord's lovingkindnesses indeed never cease,
for His compassions never fail. They are new
every morning. Great is Your faithfulness.

LAMENTATIONS 3:22–23 NASB

SEPTEMBER 12

The pure in heart are blessed,
for they will see God.

MATTHEW 5:8 HCSB

Blessed assurance; Jesus is mine!
Oh, what a foretaste of glory divine!
Heir of salvation, purchase of God,
Born of his Spirit, washed in his blood.

Blessed Assurance
FANNY CROSBY
1873

SEPTEMBER 11

Lord, I want to be a Christian in my heart, in my heart.
Lord, I want to be a Christian in my heart.
In my heart, in my heart,
Lord, I want to be a Christian in my heart.

Lord I Want to Be a Christian
TRADITIONAL SPIRITUAL

The Lord God is a sun and shield. The Lord gives grace and glory; He does not withhold the good from those who live with integrity. Happy is the person who trusts in You, Lord of Hosts!

PSALM 84:11–12 HCSB

I came that they may have life,
and have it abundantly.

JOHN 10:10 NASB

Let us draw near with a true heart
in full assurance of faith, having our hearts
sprinkled from an evil conscience
and our bodies washed with pure water.

HEBREWS 10:22 NKJV

Every day we live is a priceless gift of God,
loaded with possibilities to learn something new,
to gain fresh insights.

DALE EVANS ROGERS

If God be for us,
who can be against us?

ROMANS 8:31 KJV

I delight greatly in the Lord;
my soul rejoices in my God.

ISAIAH 61:10 NIV

Today, as you live in the present and look to the future,
remember that God is your shepherd, now and forever.
When you do, you can rest assured that this day,
like every other, is only a foretaste of glory divine.

SEPTEMBER 7

Today, like every other, is a priceless gift
from the Creator. He has offered us yet another
opportunity to serve Him with smiling faces
and willing hands. When we do our part,
He inevitably does His part, and miracles happen.

Have you not known? Have you not heard?
The everlasting God, the Lord, the Creator
of the ends of the earth, neither faints nor is weary.
His understanding is unsearchable.
He gives power to the weak, and to those
who have no might He increases strength.

ISAIAH 40:28–29 NKJV

SEPTEMBER 6

Rejoice always, pray without ceasing,
in everything give thanks; for this is the will of God
in Christ Jesus for you.

1 THESSALONIANS 5:16–18 NKJV

If you realize that there is a higher love and guidance
that comes from God, then it gives you
a peaceful feeling that no material possession
can provide. It's the assurance, down deep,
that everything is going to be all right.

TENNESSEE ERNIE FORD

Rejoice in the Lord always.
Again I will say, rejoice!

PHILIPPIANS 4:4 NKJV

God's way is perfect. All the Lord's promises
prove true. He is a shield for all
who look to Him for protection.

PSALM 18:30 NLT

SEPTEMBER 4

This is the day which the Lord has made;
let us rejoice and be glad in it.

PSALM 118:24 NASB

Happy day, happy day,
When Jesus washed my sins away!
He taught me how to watch and pray,
And live rejoicing ev'ry day.
Happy day, happy day,
When Jesus washed my sins away.

O Happy Day
PHILLIP DODDRIDGE

Sowing in the morning, sowing seeds of kindness,
Sowing in the noontide and the dewy eve;
Waiting for the harvest, and the time of reaping,
We shall come rejoicing, bringing in the sheaves.

Bringing In the Sheaves
KNOWLES SHAW
1874

If they obey and serve Him, they will spend
the rest of their days in prosperity
and their years in contentment.

JOB 36:11 NIV

Jesus said, "Don't let your hearts be troubled.
Trust in God, and trust in Me."

JOHN 14:1 NCV

APRIL 29

Those who listen to instruction will prosper;
those who trust the Lord will be joyful.

PROVERBS 16:20 NLT

Jesus does not say, "There is no storm."
He says, "I am here, do not toss, but trust."

VANCE HAVNER

I have come that they may have life,
and that they may have it more abundantly.

JOHN 10:10 NKJV

AUGUST 31

The fear of man is a snare,
but the one who trusts in the Lord is protected.

PROVERBS 29:25 HCSB

Whether you are sitting on the front porch
of a small country home or lounging in the penthouse
of the tallest building in the city, you must set
your mind and heart upon God's blessings.
When you count your blessings every day—and obey
your Creator—you'll discover that happiness is not
a commodity to be purchased; it is, instead,
the natural consequence of walking daily with God.

AUGUST 30

We Christians have every reason to live courageously.
After all, Christ has already won
the ultimate battle on the cross at Calvary.

Happiness makes a person smile,
but sadness can break a person's spirit.

PROVERBS 15:13 NCV

As Christians, we can be comforted: Whether we find ourselves at the pinnacle of the mountain or the darkest depths of the valley, God is there.

Happy is the person who has learned to rejoice in the simple and beautiful things around him.

BILLY GRAHAM

AUGUST 28

The Lord is my rock, my fortress, and my deliverer,
my God, my mountain where I seek refuge.
My shield, the horn of my salvation, my stronghold,
my refuge, and my Savior.

2 SAMUEL 22:2–3 HCSB

Joyful is the person who finds wisdom,
the one who gains understanding.

PROVERBS 3:13 NLT

Trust in the Lord with all your heart, and lean not on your own understanding; in all your ways acknowledge Him, and He shall direct your paths.

PROVERBS 3:5-6 NKJV

Onward, Christian soldiers, marching as to war,
With the cross of Jesus going on before!
Christ, the royal Master, leads against the foe;
Forward into battle, see his banner go!

Onward Christian Soldiers
SABINE BARING-GOULD AND ARTHUR SULLIVAN
1871

In quietness and trust is your strength.

ISAIAH 30:15 NASB

I called to the Lord in my distress; I called to my God. From His temple He heard my voice.

2 SAMUEL 22:7 HCSB

AUGUST 25

There's a land that is fairer than day,
And by faith we can see it afar;
For the Father waits over the way
To prepare us a dwelling place there.

Sweet By and By
JOSEPH F. WEBSTER
1875

You therefore must endure hardship
as a good soldier of Jesus Christ.

2 TIMOTHY 2:3 NKJV

Let us lay aside every weight, and the sin which so easily ensnares us, and let us run with endurance the race that is set before us.

HEBREWS 12:1 NKJV

God blesses those who patiently endure testing and temptation. Afterward they will receive the crown of life that God has promised to those who love Him.

JAMES 1:12 NLT

AUGUST 23

Forbidden fruits create many jams.

MAY 9

When we are troubled, God stands ready and willing
to protect us. Our responsibility, of course, is to ask Him
for protection. When we call upon Him in prayer,
He will answer—in His own time and in His own way.

Put on the whole armor of God,
that you may be able to stand against
the wiles of the devil.

EPHESIANS 6:11 NKJV

He heals the brokenhearted
and binds up their wounds.

PSALM 147:3 HCSB

Take a stand against the enemy,
and ask for God's protection.

Adversity is not simply a tool. It is God's most effective
tool for the advancement of our spiritual lives.
The events that we see as setbacks are oftentimes
the very things that launch us into periods
of intense spiritual growth.

CHARLES STANLEY

Encourage each other daily,
while it is still called today.

HEBREWS 3:13 HCSB

We are hard pressed on every side, yet not crushed;
we are perplexed, but not in despair.

2 CORINTHIANS 4:8 NKJV

AUGUST 19

All sore and weak from backsliding?
Try pew-sitting and knee-bends.

Come to the church in the wildwood,
Oh, come to the church in the vale.
No spot is so dear to my childhood
As the little brown church in the vale.

The Church in the Wildwood
WILLIAM S. PITTS
1857

No temptation has overtaken you but such as is common to man; and God is faithful, who will not allow you to be tempted beyond what you are able, but with the temptation will provide the way of escape.

1 CORINTHIANS 10:13 NASB

Be on guard for yourselves and for all the flock
that the Holy Spirit has appointed you
as overseers, to shepherd the church of God,
which He purchased with His own blood.

ACTS 20:28 HCSB

Ask the Savior to help you,
Comfort, strengthen and keep you;
He is willing to aid you,
He will carry you through.

Yield Not to Temptation
DR. H. R. PALMER
1868

I was glad when they said unto me,
Let us go into the house of the Lord.

PSALM 122:1 KJV

AUGUST 16

We must do the works of Him who sent Me
while it is day. Night is coming when no one can work.

JOHN 9:4 HCSB

For where two or three gather in My name,
there am I with them.

MATTHEW 18:20 NIV

It is true that we may desire much more.
But let us use what we have,
and God will give us more.

ADONIRAM JUDSON

Every church, regardless of its size, needs dedicated parishioners who understand the importance of sustaining—and being sustained by—their local congregations. In the Book of Acts, Luke instructs us to "feed the church of God"(20:28). As Christians who have been given so much by our loving heavenly Father, we should worship Him not only in our hearts but also in the presence of fellow believers.

AUGUST 14

By their fruits ye shall know them.

MATTHEW 7:20 KJV

MAY 18

Enter His gates with thanksgiving,
go into His courts with praise.
Give thanks to Him and praise His name.

PSALM 100:4 NLT

Sometimes, when we are tired or discouraged, our worries can sap our strength and sidetrack our motivation. But God has other intentions. He expects us to work for the things that we pray for. More importantly, God intends that our work should become His work.

The church is where it's at.
The first place of Christian service
for any Christian is in a local church.

JERRY CLOWER

AUGUST 12

He said to His disciples,
"The harvest is abundant,
but the workers are few."

MATTHEW 9:37 HCSB

God is Spirit, and those who worship Him
must worship in spirit and truth.

JOHN 4:24 HCSB

AUGUST 11

So then, each of us will give
an account of himself to God.

ROMANS 14:12 HCSB

Jesus loves me, this I know,
For the Bible tells me so.
Little ones to Him belong;
They are weak, but He is strong.

Jesus Loves Me
ANNA BARTLETT WARNER
1860

AUGUST 10

Better to be patient than powerful;
better to have self-control than to conquer a city.

PROVERBS 16:32 NLT

I am the good shepherd. The good shepherd gives His life for the sheep.

JOHN 10:11 NKJV

Blessed Savior, Thou wilt guide us,
Till we reach the blissful shore,
Where the angels wait to join us
In Thy praise forevermore.

Life's Railroad to Heaven
M. E. ABBEY AND CHARLIE D. TILLMAN
1891

The next day John saw Jesus coming toward him and said, "Here is the Lamb of God, who takes away the sin of the world!"

JOHN 1:29 HCSB

Now the God of all grace, who called you
to His eternal glory in Christ Jesus, will personally
restore, establish, strengthen, and support you.

1 PETER 5:10 HCSB

I have come as a light into the world,
that whoever believes in Me
should not abide in darkness.

JOHN 12:46 NKJV

God is not running an antique shop!
He is making all things new!

VANCE HAVNER

Christ's love endures. Even when we falter, He loves us. When we fall prey to the world's temptations, He remains steadfast. When we make mistakes, He forgives us completely. In fact, no power on earth can separate us from His love.

Finally, brothers, rejoice. Become mature,
be encouraged, be of the same mind, be at peace,
and the God of love and peace will be with you.

2 CORINTHIANS 13:11 HCSB

Who can separate us from the love of Christ? Can affliction or anguish or persecution or famine or nakedness or danger or sword? ...No, in all these things we are more than victorious through Him who loved us.

ROMANS 8:35, 37 HCSB

AUGUST 5

For busy citizens of the 21st century, it's easy
to become overcommitted, overworked, over-stressed,
and overwhelmed. If we choose, we can be connected 24-7,
sparing just enough time to a few hours' sleep each night.
What we need is time to renew and recharge, but where
can we find the time? We can find it with God.

Jesus—the standard of measurement,
the scale of weights, the test of character
for the whole moral universe.

R. G. LEE

Remember ye not the former things,
neither consider the things of old.
Behold, I will do a new thing.

ISAIAH 43:18–19 KJV

The thief's purpose is to steal and kill and destroy.
My purpose is to give them a rich and satisfying life.

JOHN 10:10 NLT

Therefore, if anyone is in Christ, he is a new creation;
old things have passed away;
behold, all things have become new.

2 CORINTHIANS 5:17 NKJV

This little light of mine, I'm gonna let it shine.
This little light of mine, I'm gonna let it shine.
This little light of mine, I'm gonna let it shine,
Let it shine, let it shine, let it shine.

This Little Light of Mine
TRADITIONAL SPIRITUAL

Those who hope in the Lord will renew their strength. They will soar on wings like eagles; they will run and not grow weary, they will walk and not be faint.

ISAIAH 40:31 NIV

MAY 30

I have come as a light into the world, so that everyone who believes in Me would not remain in darkness.

JOHN 12:46 HCSB

Softly and tenderly Jesus is calling,
Calling for you and for me;
See, on the portals He's waiting and watching,
Watching for you and for me.

Softly and Tenderly Jesus Is Calling
WILL L. THOMPSON
1880

This is the message which we have heard from Him
and declare to you, that God is light
and in Him is no darkness at all.

1 JOHN 1:5 NKJV

JULY 31

And we have known and believed the love that God has for us. God is love, and he who abides in love abides in God, and God in him.

1 JOHN 4:16 NKJV

You were once darkness, but now you are light in the Lord. Walk as children of light—for the fruit of the light results in all goodness, righteousness, and truth—discerning what is pleasing to the Lord.

EPHESIANS 5:8–10 HCSB

We need more love for the word
and less love for the world.

R. G. LEE

Every day, we make decisions that can bring us closer to God, or not. When we follow closely in the footsteps of Christ, we experience His blessings and His peace. When we live in the light, we serve as a powerful example and a positive role model in a world that surely needs both.

Above all, love each other deeply,
because love covers a multitude of sins.

1 PETER 4:8 NIV

Lord, You are my lamp;
the Lord illuminates my darkness.

2 SAMUEL 22:29 HCSB

"'Love the Lord your God with all your heart and with all your soul and with all your mind.' This is the first and greatest commandment. And the second is like it: 'Love your neighbor as yourself.' All the Law and the Prophets hang on these two commandments"(Matthew 22:37-40 NIV). We are commanded to love the One who first loved us and then to share His love with the world.

We must always invite Jesus to be the navigator
of our plans, desires, wills, and emotions,
for He is the way, the truth, and the life.

BILL BRIGHT

JULY 27

Love is patient, love is kind. Love does not envy, is not boastful, is not conceited.

1 CORINTHIANS 13:4 HCSB

You are the light that gives light to the world....
In the same way, you should be a light for other people.
Live so that they will see the good things you do
and will praise your Father in heaven.

MATTHEW 5:14, 16 NCV

And now abide faith, hope, love, these three;
but the greatest of these is love.

1 CORINTHIANS 13:13 NKJV

Nearer, my God, to thee, nearer to thee!
E'en though it be a cross that raiseth me,
Still all my song shall be, nearer, my God, to thee;
Nearer, my God, to thee, nearer to thee!

Nearer, My God to Thee
SARAH FLOWERS ADAMS
1805-1848

JULY 25

A new commandment I give unto you,
that ye love one another; as I have loved you,
that ye also love one another.

JOHN 13:34 KJV

Draw near to God,
and He will draw near to you.

JAMES 4:8 HCSB

Love lifted me! Love lifted me!
When nothing else could help,
Love lifted me.
Love lifted me! Love lifted me!
When nothing else could help,
Love lifted me.

Love Lifted Me
JAMES ROWE
1912

The eyes of Yahweh roam throughout the earth
to show Himself strong for those
whose hearts are completely His.

2 CHRONICLES 16:9 HCSB

You also have sorrow now.
But I will see you again.
Your hearts will rejoice,
and no one will rob you of your joy.

JOHN 16:22 HCSB

I know the Lord is always with me.
I will not be shaken, for He is right beside me.

PSALM 16:8 NLT

There is not one blade of grass, there is no color
in this world that is not intended to make us rejoice.

JOHN CALVIN

God's love is infinite. His love spans the entirety of His creation. His love touches the far reaches of His vast universe as well as the quiet corners of every human heart.

Until now you have asked for nothing in My name.
Ask and you will receive, that your joy may be complete.

JOHN 16:24 HCSB

Though I walk through the valley of the shadow of death, I will fear no evil: for Thou art with me.

PSALM 23:4 KJV

The joy that the world offers is fleeting and incomplete: here today, gone tomorrow, not coming back anytime soon. But God's joy is different. His joy has staying power. In fact, it's a gift that never stops giving to those who welcome His Son into their hearts.

The knowledge that we are never alone
calms the troubled sea of our lives
and speaks peace to our souls.

A. W. TOZER

I have spoken these things to you so that My joy may be in you and your joy may be complete.

JOHN 15:11 HCSB

I am not alone,
because the Father is with Me.

JOHN 16:32 NKJV

JULY 18

This is the day which the LORD has made;
let us rejoice and be glad in it.

PSALM 118:24 NASB

Yes, we'll gather at the river,
The beautiful, the beautiful river;
Gather with the saints at the river
That flows by the throne of God.

Shall We Gather at the River?
ROBERT LOWERY
1763

Rejoice always, pray without ceasing,
in everything give thanks; for this is the will of God
in Christ Jesus for you.

1 THESSALONIANS 5:16–18 NKJV

I assure you: Anyone who hears My word
and believes Him who sent Me has eternal life
and will not come under judgment
but has passed from death to life.

JOHN 5:24 HCSB

Joyful, joyful, we adore You, God of glory, Lord of love;
Hearts unfold like flow'rs before You,
op'ning to the sun above.
Melt the clouds of sin and sadness;
drive the dark of doubt away;
Giver of immortal gladness,
fill us with the light of day!

Joyful, Joyful, We Adore Thee
HENRY VAN DYKE
1911

For God so loved the world, that He gave
His only begotten Son, that whosoever believeth in Him
should not perish, but have everlasting life.

JOHN 3:16 KJV

Ask, and it will be given to you; seek, and you will find; knock, and it will be opened to you. For everyone who asks receives, and he who seeks finds, and to him who knocks it will be opened.

MATTHEW 7:7–8 NASB

For the wages of sin is death, but the gift of God is eternal life in Christ Jesus our Lord.

ROMANS 6:23 NIV

We honor God by asking for great things when they are a part of His promise. We dishonor Him and cheat ourselves when we ask for molehills where He has promised mountains.

VANCE HAVNER

Jesus is not only the light of the world; He is also its salvation. He came to this earth so that we might not perish, but instead spend eternity with Him. What a glorious gift; what a priceless opportunity.

Whenever you stand praying, if you have anything against anyone, forgive him, so that your Father in heaven will also forgive you your wrongdoing.

MARK 11:25 HCSB

I have written these things to you who believe
in the name of the Son of God, so that you may know
that you have eternal life.

1 JOHN 5:13 HCSB

No matter where you happen to be, whether you're in the city, the suburbs, the country, or anyplace in between, you always have a lifeline to God. Prayer is a powerful tool that you can use to change your world and change yourself.

When ten thousand times ten thousand
times ten thousand years have passed,
eternity will have just begun.

BILLY SUNDAY

Confess your trespasses to one another, and pray for one another, that you may be healed. The effective, fervent prayer of a righteous man avails much.

JAMES 5:16 NKJV

The world and its desires pass away,
but the man who does the will of God lives forever.

1 JOHN 2:17 NIV

Rejoice always, pray without ceasing,
in everything give thanks; for this is the will of God
in Christ Jesus for you.

1 THESSALONIANS 5:16-18 NKJV

The Lord is my shepherd; I shall not want.
He makes me to lie down in green pastures;
He leads me beside the still waters.
He restores my soul;
He leads me in the paths of righteousness
For His name's sake.

THE 23RD PSALM

Is anyone among you suffering?
He should pray.

JAMES 5:13 HCSB

I will lift up mine eyes unto the hills,
from whence cometh my help.

PSALM 121:1 KJV

Sweet hour of prayer! Sweet hour of prayer!
That calls me from a world of care,
And bids me at my Father's throne
Make all my wants and wishes known.

Sweet Hour of Prayer
W. W. WALFORD
1845

Surely goodness and mercy shall follow me
all the days of my life: and I will dwell
in the house of the Lord for ever.

PSALM 23:6 KJV

To every thing there is a season...
a time to keep silence, and a time to speak.

ECCLESIASTES 3:1, 7 KJV

In God, whose word I praise—
in God I trust and am not afraid.

PSALM 56:4 NIV

The prayer offered to God in the morning
during your quiet time is the key
that unlocks the door of the day.

ADRIAN ROGERS

JUNE 26

On occasion, you will endure circumstances that break your heart and test your faith. When you are fearful, trust in God. When you are anxious, turn your worries over to Him. When you are unsure of your next step, be still and listen carefully for the Lord's guidance. And then place your life in His hands. He is your shepherd today, tomorrow, and forever.

In quietness and in confidence shall be your strength.

ISAIAH 30:15 KJV

It is good for me to draw near to God:
I have put my trust in the Lord God.

PSALM 73:28 KJV

Today and every day, you need quiet, uninterrupted time alone with God. You need to be still and listen for His voice. And, you need to seek His guidance in matters great and small. Your Creator has important plans for your day and your life.

JUNE 28

As you walk through the valley of the unknown,
you will find the footprints of Jesus
both in front of you and beside you.

CHARLES STANLEY

Be still, and know that I am God.

PSALM 46:10 KJV

He said: "The Lord is my rock and my fortress and my deliverer; the God of my strength, in whom I will trust."

2 SAMUEL 22:2–3 NKJV

JULY 2

Now in the morning, having risen a long while
before daylight, He went out and departed
to a solitary place; and there He prayed.

MARK 1:35 NKJV

JUNE 30

And He walks with me, and He talks with me,
And He tells me I am His own,
And the joy we share as we tarry there,
None other has ever known.

I Come to the Garden Alone
C. AUSTIN MILES
1912

JULY 1

Truly my soul silently waits for God;
from Him comes my salvation.

PSALM 62:1 NKJV